D0776102

It's A Lonely Love

Hunter Summerall

Andrews McMeel
PUBLISHING®

TRIGGER WARNING:

Poems included in the following work discuss
depression and suicidal ideation and could
have a triggering effect for those dealing with
traumatic experiences or mental health issues.

Falling

EVERY WAY

you were beautiful.

in every way
possible and impossible.

APPARITION

you move as a ghost does,
so ethereal and graceful.
an apparition.

most could only see
if you allowed it, but
my eyes could never leave you.

WANT TO SEE?

i need you
so much more than you know.

i could show you.

some day in some life
when you show me
that you want to be shown.

A HEART SOMEWHERE

there are so many hearts
that might say or do
what i refuse.

and they must be so
alive.

PERILOUS

refraining submission
to someone who may
open new parts of you—better parts—
takes a lot of strength,
but is far from courageous.
it's a perilous form of fear
to give in to.

EMPTY GIVINGS

i'm afraid that i'll let you
ruin everything i've
become and it all will be for
nothing when nothing
is all you will have to give.

READ

i wish that one day you'll be able to understand
how long i've waited to feel this with someone like you.

it's alive in my eyes and has been written on my lips.

you just need to learn how to read it.
you will and i'll wait.

WHERE THE WHISPERS ARE

all those love stories and movies
i wanted to understand;
i now know how oblivious i was to what
exactly i was trying to feel.

i thought maybe my feelings were too dead
or maybe even alive as living can be
and the feeling of love really was
just what i could only see.

you've taught me so much.

my only dire wish now is that
i could thank you
and show you what you have shown me.

until then, until maybe never,
or until maybe even tomorrow,
the only love i've yet to know will
remain in my veins where the whispers are quietest
and you cannot hear
unless you were searching,
feeling.

TRIPPING ON YOU

keen ears
when you're gone.
listening
to the loudest silence
to find you.

my ears ring
and i max that Delicate volume.

we're dancing in my head
to your favorite colors.
i'm tripping over our feet.

i'm falling.
don't leave me dancing alone,
i'm tripping for you.

IN YOUR DEBT FOREVER

the amount of knowledge you could give me
with just one touch of your lips against mine
is inconceivable.

give me just one and enlighten me with
what i have never understood before and

i'll be in your debt forever.

ONLY OURS

and then you were mine.

i had always been yours, but somehow
you then became mine and
i finally had the only Ours that i needed.

Flying

ALWAYS IN MY HEAD

the next day when
my feet run to you,

my arms come to you
and my hands feel for you.

my head hasn't anything to change.
and we kiss.

MY TIME

be here and be my time
for when time takes me away
i will still be where
i belong.

CASKET

be my casket.

wrap your arms around me
as i still.

NOTHING WAS YOU

i didn't realize what i was feeling
for you
until i lay in my bed
and felt as if half of it
were missing.

my arms were burdened with the strongest
urge to wrap around something,
but nothing was you.

SOCKS

sleeping without you
is so weird.

walking on
an ice cap without shoes
when my feet can't find yours.

nobody wants that.

i think i'll just stay
in your bed.
keep my feet close
to yours.

my favorite pair of socks.

LOUD

everything just kind of stops moving
with you.

everything around us,
everything in my head.

the surrealism scares me, but i crave it.

it all becomes so quiet
and i hear something so loud.

i don't know if it's the way you look at me after
or maybe it's my heart,
but i hope you hear it, too.

HAPPY SHADES

alone on this roof with you
felt like a world alone itself.

just you and i entranced in the sight over edge.
city buildings, blurry cars, and street lights.
smog, too.
i can smell the pollution.

the trees came next, piling higher
up the growing mountains
leaving our lonesome world,
reaching to find another
while the sun lowers into the horizon
guiding their way.

sunlight shimmers and our city lights swim around
the pollution, sure to enrapture anyone's eye.
pretty things painting the grand, foul remnant.

you wanted to run with them,
searching for a new world.
you found a solacing beauty in this,
knowing you could.

i watched in your eyes.
shades of orange and happiness.

UNKNOWN KNOWINGS

to drown the unknown knowings of
the undoable doings i have done
has been all i've known.

but i now know in me, through you,
i feel more.

something that frees me of my hell.

I ENJOYED THE NIGHT

once upon a time
i enjoyed the night.
it spoke of the most fascinating tales.

now it tells me the time
for you to leave is near.

CONSTELLATING

oh,
i can feel the stars
when you kiss me there.

do it again,
build another

let's float in this
time-absented constellation.

oh,
i can feel the stars
when you kiss me everywhere.

A PLACE OF NOTHING

you hid yourself from this world,
as did i, but somehow
we found one another—in a place of nothing, i assume.

because to you i was just all there was.
to me, you were all i wanted.
you welcomed me with a mind so luring.

you had a beauty that anyone could see
and then you had a beauty only i can feel.

WORDS

i never felt the weight of words
before we met.

they're so heavy.

MAYBE EVEN TOO MUCH

i don't feel usually,
but when i am with you
i feel everything.

why must i be in love
to feel something.

why must my way to feel
one thing at all be the way
i feel everything at once.

maybe even too much,
but i never want it
to be any less
and never will it ever.

NECESSARY

wasting time is what we're best at.
it's just so easy together,
but please don't waste the time i use to make ours
    matter.

GOOD MORNING TO THE BOTH OF YOU

poured my heart into some messages.
thought it would be cute when you woke.

turns out,
you were already awake with him
when you got my 2am text.

it's too late to put it all back in
so here i lie,
dumb again.
feeling dirtier than you.

Fallacy

it's a lonely love

NEW SIDES

plays switched and
new sides exist.

either pull or release, i cry.

and what was Ours started
to feel like only mine.

TRAINWRECK

i see what's coming for me.
i have been tied to these tracks before.

different station,
different train,
same destination.

i'm not alone in your head,
i'm aware.
but it's worse that
i thought i was in your heart.

FLY HIM TO THE MOON

i stood there waiting for that
door to open, every time it swung,
for you to walk out
and continued until
you did.

except,
it never was.
not exactly.

a life-form painted over
in my head to see instead of you.
nothing more,
anymore.

i lie in your bed knowing
you lie to my heart.
you were elsewhere,
flying to the moon with him.

FLY HIM TO THE MOON: SEQUEL

i tried my best to show you the
beauty of this place.
i wish i could've made yours better,
the way you told me i did.

i only ever sought your happiness.
and you told me you found it easiest
together.
it was all you ever wanted.

we rotate and revolve
with what's around us and
i orbited around the lies you fed me.

though Ours wasn't enough.
you needed his, too.
but you said to me you needed Ours and i stayed in
    orbit
until i was an earth-bound rocket left behind.

POT OF GOLD

you're chasing a rainbow.
it's only a myth, dear.
there is no pot.

i mean,
i'm chasing you so
what is my opinion worth
anyways.

STILL HERE

i can still smell you on my skin
and taste you on my lips.

i still want you and i still need you
and i'm still yours
so stay mine for me, and for you
if need be.

i'm still here.

OUR STARS

our futures aren't aligned.
but who knows what our stars might do.

EXCHANGES

exchanges of words and phrases and
the passing of sentences and replies with answers and
repeat,
yet no conversation of true heart is spoken.

though, pure intention is made,
for without the sound of your voice, thoughts, or
presence inside my head—ruining inside my body—
all these words and phrases and passing of sentences
will have no beginning to repeat
and nothing to feel.

my desires will envy the rate
of which my entire being comes nearer
to an emotional state of absence where
feeling you again only exists in a parallel form
with no chance of collision.

however, there is death which is merciful
and would offer peace and the honor
of ending the possibility of only turning right.

no thanks.

TOO HEAVY

when did i become too heavy
for this frozen ground?

why do my steps continue to break
what holds me up?

is it that i carry too much with me;
the suffering and mistakes?

everything i ever do is breaking.

WANT ME

i've known from the beginning
that you never
needed me.

you don't need anyone
and that's beautiful.

i just always hoped that you
wanted me.

GUT OVER EARS

a second choice since
the first time.

i trust my gut
more than my ears.

your words are weaker
than your head and
quieter than your thoughts.

SORROW RAINS

the sorrow is raining.
the drainage pipes are broken.

sadness falls and the
breathing is dying.

circles never change.

OUR MATTERS START MATTERING

show me you're not fading.
show me you still care.
show me i'm still yours.
show me everything.

let our matters start mattering
once more.

FEELING LIKE YOU

my toes to yours,
we step.

your lips to mine,
we dance.

the beat in me skips
and it's feeling
like you.

SO COLD

that heat you inflicted that kept me warm
burns an agonizing pain.

it could be the icing of
my own from becoming so cold.

either way,
i've grown numb to anything
other than this wound.

BUTTERFLY BLOOD

your name
lights up my phone,

my nerves tickle
my blood

and the disease grows.

UNCHANGING

moments of despair
flash across my life
every now and then.

like when i realized
nothing changed when i thought
all the change
was unchanging.

SHIVERING SHEETS

i long for the night
my blankets are cozy again
without you in them.

FOUNDATIONS

the slightest thought ever imaginable
of any amounted time with you,
no matter how small or large,
that we have not spent together
is tearing every part of me from
the inside out.

but every spark inside of me you give
is worth the unending promises i crave in my heart.

they're slowing killing the foundations
of everything i am and i'm too weak to run away.

hunter summerall

HIGH TIDE STARS

atop a sand castle,
howling into space
to shoot us a star.
wishing the high tide
won't catch us in time.

INTENTIONS

i can feel your hands
when you feel him.

only it's in my head and the intentions
aren't where i wish them to be.

i'm self-destructing.

GRAY OCEANS

every memory,
every dream,
every desire and hope
i ever had with or for you and for us,
replays over and over in my head.

give me some kind of an ending.

i'd much rather take the truth
to end it all
than suffer cycles of pain
because this hasn't stopped
and it's all in your hands.

please.

or give me a sequel
of fulfilled desires and hopes.
or take it all back.
take it all away or give me everything.

treading in gray oceans
is so tiresome and i'm exhausted.

BURNT MY TONGUE

coffee held in my hands
still hot, still full.
i wonder,
how many others do you do
this with?

do they order what i do?
the order you gave me.

for some reason i thought
it was ours.

but i also thought,
for some reason,
you loved only
me.

turns out i was crazy to think
you loved me at all.
but i really
thought you loved me.

i burnt my tongue again.

IT'S SO DARK HERE

the depth of your lies feels so deep
and it is so dark here.

i just keep waiting for hell to consume.
i guess this is all there is.

maybe this is our eternity i'm stuck with.

IN THE END

everything will be
okay in the end.

i will be happy
or i will be dead and feel
nothing.

i won't even exist
except in the memories
of those i've marked
and i hope your heart is scarred.

FALLING TREES

i want to be a tree
that falls in love with
the earth, not the sun.

FEBRUARY NONSENSE

february days feel
like midsummer.

our grass yellows,
not like it should
from the snow,
but from the sun.

my pain comes from you,
not like it should,
but it does.

nothing is right.

i miss the playground
scrapes and bruises
and my Band-Aids
to fix them.

PROPHECY

i hope these creatures of
inevitability, bound by their
false fables, learn to change
their prewritten fates
and save themselves from what
ultimately will become of them.

YOU KNOW WHAT YOU DO

you weren't someone to mess around with.

the simplest touch could
ruin everything i knew.
sometimes i wonder if you know your harm.

of course you do.

you know what you do
and you love it.
you live for it.
you thrive on it.

CIVIL WAR

we used to be unbeatable,
always surviving the bored.

we could've conquered all we wanted.

broken by our civil war,
we've wasted everything
at each other's throats.

NIGHT SKIES

the night creeps into my mind again while i lie in bed.
the ominous thoughts and nightmares
should start settling in before i even fall asleep,
but tonight seems to be different.

i'm falling into this abyss inside my head
filled with images of you and i can't make them go
     away.

i wish my roof were gone
so i could lose my thoughts into the stars.

then i got to thinking about every freckle
intricately designed on your skin,
like the stars in my night sky i so wish to see.

that's when i realized there could be no escape.
i hated you for it.

THIRSTY FEELINGS

i sip to suppress,
though it seems my thoughts
have developed feelings of
their own.

they take offense and rampage,
setting fires,
havoc to the others.

it's a contagious disarray
beyond my control.

i, the tragic hero of my own tale,
giving sovereignty to
an arrow aimed for my heel.

THE NOISES OF YOUR INTIMACY

i feel you when you feel him,
it's all in my head as if it were me.

i hear the noises
of your intimacy and affection.
it sounds terribly similar
to my pain.

i can feel every feel you feel
and it burns.

VOCAL ADDICT

i know what personification is.
i've seen it in film and
read it in writing.

i've never heard it like this.
i hurt, and it's your voice.

it's messing me up because
hurting sucks.
it really does.
but it sounds like you
and your voice is addicting.

i'm addicted to being hurt.

ALMOST

i was almost good.
almost.

FLATLINE

i find it awfully hard to understand that someone
could make me feel the way you did,
treat me as you did,
then act as if it never existed.

as if our hearts never pulsed against one another
beneath our chests.

but you do and my beat weakens.

EVER DYING LOVE

round two,
still dead.

took a few breaths,
but still dead
and still dying.

STORY OF US

your absence has kept me
from writing.

i want to.
i want to write our story into your head.
into your mind and soul,
into your veins.

i want to write our story of us not only
so i will be happy, but so
i will be in control of who is killed.

neither of us needs to cry.

SAVIOR

when armies were at my throat
and i couldn't fight,
i trusted in you for salvation.

here i cry from the grave.

INTERRUPTED LOVE LIGHTS

i see things in lights a lot
and lights don't just end.
they're continuous unless obstructed.

i love you the way a light works.
it's continuous and if this
obstruction were gone,
i promise you'd still see it.

MY BLOOD, MY LUNGS

i'm walking down some sidewalk
on the street.

bottle in hand,
and you're everywhere.

the taint in my blood,
the tears in my lungs.

nothing kills me faster than you.

COPPER

i crave your hand pressed against my face.
i miss the feeling of it against my cheek.

i hold mine there wishing yours never left, and
tears dampen my skin.

i can taste the copper.
my reflection is streaked in red
where your fingers lay.

i can't even look away.

JUST MYSELF

i'm so alone again,
at least i had someone last time.

but no, i just have myself.

i don't even know who i am anymore
so what good is that.

MOTHER

this is something not even
a mother's calming love can soothe.

CARCINOGENS

i mistook the glowing ember
i saw you as, hanging from my mouth,
for a raging fire bringing life into me.

now i see that you were only a cigarette
and i breathed you in too quickly.
you burned out by my own doing and
i was left with only chemicals inside.

now when i think of you, i light a cigarette
and watch the glowing ember thrive,
bringing back memories of you and me,
and i let it fall to the ground
wishing i had never
held you between my lips.

STOLEN

we were criminals on the run
from our own hostile organs.
my head, your heart.

it was a failed heist
we ran from and we never
learned to stop.
running in our own ways,
separate ways,
to others, from others,
from our own selves.

CORRIDORS

isn't it peculiar to think
about how much clearer you see
in the dark?

a horrifying place it can be, yes,
but when so little light is
left to be hopeful for,
it really opens up boundaries
your thoughts haven't known.

miraculous corridors of the wicked.

the most terrifying form of
enlightenment you will ever experience.

SLEEPING IGNORANTLY

why does being awake
have to be so unfortunate.

DREAMING

i think it would be nice
to just not wake up.

people tell me,

"to die before
living your dreams is
the saddest tragedy."

what if i stayed in them forever?

LAUGH WITH ME

so much laughter in the halls.
so much laughter.
where can i learn that while stuck
in here.
i envy the feeling.

LIE UNDER

time is rolling,
time to lie under,
time to learn,
and time to end.

CONTROLLER

i get told all the time that
it's in my head.

it's not.
it's everywhere.

my chest, my gut,
my hands, the air,
my bed.

it's not something i can control
without you.

it's a lonely love

NO SURFACE

no matter how hard
i push off the floor of this ocean,

it's never enough to
reach the surface and breathe.

I'M ECHOING

my echoes chase me around
and around my echoes take me.

how am i ever surprised anymore,
it's shocking.

it's a lonely love

LAMP

the flickering lamppost
in this parking lot began mocking me.

i get it.
neither of us have much left.

unlike you, i don't have someone
to come around and fix me.

IDK

i'm never completely okay
because i never completely know
why i'm not.

i'm ready to let go, but
i don't know how.

i don't know a lot anymore.

NEW YEAR'S KISS

between a clock and a wall,
i got my New Year's Kiss.
time has never struck midnight so long before.

i saw everything.
the kisses, the tears, the dancing,
the smiles, the pain,
the happy, our future.
everything.

eyes closed, slow dancing with you.
my soul dancing with yours.

you could only see another kiss.
another dance.
you see the person you were with
the night before
and thinking of who you'll see
the night after.

i should've died in the longest midnight.
save me the naivety,
i've become enough, it seems.

so sorry to me.

SHORTAGE

found a couple photos
that fell beneath my desk.

an age of reminiscence found.

a short age i dream of
that has me damned for life.

I MISS OURS

i miss being your only one
and i miss making you happy.

i miss Ours and now it's just mine.

it's a lonely love.

NOT YOU

sure, i've kissed a lot of lips,
held several hands,
but what does it matter to me
if it's not you.

RIDE

any emotion for another
frightens me like a new ride
i'm not strapped in for.

the nausea from the last
hasn't settled.
it's a hard sickness.

WASTE CONTRIBUTION

so much precious time
and precious life wasted on
a lost soul for a lost love.

if i had known how deep
i would be left to die,
i wouldn't have lended a hand.

LIFE TIME

every night at 6:16
i would remind myself of this
gift i carry called Life.

i hardly care to
check the time anymore.

SUNKEN WINGS

let's run here, you ran there
and we watched
all your favorite movies.
i'll watch mine later, i guess.

we never got to
look at my favorite
section of the bookstore.
i hope you enjoy the books you got.

i wanted frozen yogurt,
you wanted johnny
rockets.
the milkshake was good, it's cool.

these things are okay.
i never minded.

i can love
the things
you love.
i wanted to.

but i also wanted to fly.
and you made me sink.

it's a lonely love

INEVITABILITY

trees blow,
the wind sways,
we're all going to die.

SKIPPY THOUGHTS

bright eyes and smiles have filled
the room and it's clouding my head.
their joy skips in circles around me,
emphasizing my brokenness
as i sit alone,
finding ways to cope with my demons
through words in this journal.

why was i not made to be like them?
and if i was, how have i strayed
myself so terribly far and become
what i have?

i need answers for why i am
the way i am.
why i can't be the way i wish to be.

RECYCLE

i don't know how much more i can take.

a play toy for the entertainment of selfishness.

three years of continuous use.
thrown away and recycled for more.

i don't know how much longer i can be
made new for someone before
everything gives in and i go out.

DEAR WHOM IT APPLIES,

"let it go."
"move on."
"you're better off on your own."
"you'll get over it."

yes, well then screw you.

i can't let go of something i don't
even have a hold of.

i can't move on if i don't even know
where i am.

if i am better off on my own then
why am i this way.

let me bear what i feel instead
of telling me i can
change what i actually can't,
as if i willingly chose this desolation.

if i will get over it then so be it, but i am not.
so screw you and screw off.

BROKEN BODY

a bone doesn't heal because
you tell it to.

it heals in time
and in that time you have to
bear the pain.
bear the consequence.

you adapt to life with it.
you learn what makes it easier
until it is better.

i can't be over this because i say i am.
but i will be in time.
and i will adapt.

HOLIDAY FROSTBITE

being in love with you
is being in the snow of the
holiday season, drinking
hot chocolate,
open-toed in summer clothes.

filling moments of warmth
in me when i drink.
pleasurable, though fleeting,
my body still becomes
frostbitten.

DELUGE

the circles you drew into
the back of my neck spin.

i miss your touch.

your cheek against my cheek,
the gifts your lips leave down
my face on the way to mine.

i miss your skin.

i try so hard to dam the rivers,
but the fear shakes.

i'm flooding myself until
i drown for you.

GREEN FLASH

i saw you for the first time
since our last time.

i watched him touch the lips
that have left scars all over my body.

i watched him watch you like he's seeing
the sun lie under
the ocean for the first time
and i watched you look at him.

you look at him and wait to disappear
and you'll be gone
before he even sees the flash of green.

COMES AND GOES

you don't care,
you don't consider,
and you don't really love.

i promise it's okay.
it always comes and goes.

DIFFERENT NOW

i was dumb to give my whole heart
and self to something
i didn't understand called love.

but i also know it didn't matter
to me at the time when i felt the way i did.

nothing else mattered and i thought
that was the beauty of it.

and still, nothing else does matter,
but it's different now.

DROWN ME

i know i still love you, despite this pain,
because when i smell the things that were ours
i'm overcome with a drowning rush of vivid memories
that feel nice like it once did the original time.

it's when the rush passes moments
after that rips me inside out.

if i could drown in that rush forever with you,
i would never hurt again.

LESSER

they tell me i will fall in love again
one day and forget about you and this pain.

but i don't want to.

no love will feel like yours did
because no other love is your love.

i'd rather keep burning in this hell
with the memory of your touch
than forget it to a lesser substitution
that will eventually
result in the same cycle of pain.

SMELL LIKE ME

you came back to bed
smelling like his.

i'm glad i don't smell
like you anymore.

TEMPORARY

i tell myself nothing is forever.

we were the one thing
that i was so sure
could achieve it and didn't.

so even when i feel
like all this aching will
never cease to exist and i wish
that i, myself, could,
i know i can't.

if the only forever i ever knew,
was temporary,
then i know this suffering will be, too.

KEEP LIVING

i still feel lost, however,
i am finding more of myself every day.

i've been slowly finding ways to come back together
and be me again.

i will still hurt because i still love you.

that's not something i can see ever changing,
but i am healing.

i know how to live with it now and i will keep living.

US AGAIN

as bizarre as hating someone
you love sounds, it's possible.
i love you, still.

i would do anything to have our love
be ours again, but i hate you
so much for doing this.

i don't want to hate you,
just like i don't want to love you, but
i can't help the overwhelming repulsion
that envelops me when
i think of you and this curse.

i can't deny that you
could take it all away
and fix this mess you've made of me
and i can't deny that i would forgive you.

as much shame as it brings me to admit,
i would do anything you asked
and give anything of me that you need
for us again.

ME BEFORE YOU

i think that if i give up then
i'll eventually get past you.

i just don't know how long it'll take.
or how bad it will hurt.

but i know the few breaths
i share with you outweigh the pain.

and that's why i'm moving on.
you're an addictive toxin
that's just going to kill me
and i need to love me more than you

so i move on.

Feat

MISGUIDED THEORY

acatalepsy,
an old word i heard about once.

something about the impossibility
to comprehend the universe.
that it's too complex and vast
for human knowledge which has
no real true certainty anyways,
making the infinite solutions to the
universe that much more impossible
to comprehend.

in other words:
trying to explain how much
i love you.

how much i *thought* i loved you.

WAYWARD DESPAIR

midnight revelations,
realizations,
of repressed thoughts.
truths.

spare me, Despair.
you lost my loss.

where we were was wayward.
i found mine, find yours.

ICARUS

we were to head east
for a new life
for us.

i told myself,
you were going to
meet me halfway
when i found myself
flying alone.

you were never good with
directions.

or i'm a fool.

then
you let me fly
too close to the sun
while it shone its most beautiful.

MEMORIES HURT, HURT MEMORIES BUILD

i never thought the memory of someone
could be so dangerous.

nothing tempts me to hurt myself
the way you hurt me
more than the thought of you.

but
nothing tempts me to build myself
the way i aspire to be
more than the thought of
being hurt by you.

MATH PROBLEMS

sometimes in math class learning a new concept can be
    complicated.
sometimes it just seems more complicated than it really
    is.
like those days you repeat a problem several times
convinced you made no mistake,
but the incorrect solution you've gathered remains.

after so many attempts, something switches, turning on
    a bulb, catching your eye.
you know what's wrong and how to fix it.
you forgot to transfer your negative, subtracted wrong,
    left out a zero, whatever.
the smallest misstep overlooked again and again,
drove you so astray.

you're incredulous how you let yourself make this
    simple mistake.
how could you fall into such a mess of numbers?
you're questions behind and you're mad for wasting
so much time on a dumb thing you did.

but the thing is—it's not a dumb thing you did.
it wasn't that simple when you were learning it.
only now that you know, it has become simple to you.

you needed time, trial and error.
this is like that.
a sense of clarity snapped into place within a blink's
    moment.

i don't find myself stupid and blind.
i don't regret or feel time has been wasted on a dumb,
  simple thing.
i was learning and now i've learned.
now i know.

RECYCLE PT. 2

three years.
a play toy for the entertainment
of selfishness.

toss aside,
recycle,
toss aside,
recycle,
repeat.

part of me hates myself for allowing it,
as if i needed you like you said i did.

i don't.
it was hard to get it, but i do
now.

the air is cleaner,
lighter.
the sun is charming,
the trees are healthy,
and i'm better.

MOON CHOOSING

choose your own moons
and don't let go easily.

but let go easily when it's
best for you.

RIGHTFUL SELF-LOVE

You are the only person
You can ever have
at all points of Your life.

give You appreciation.
give You attention and treats.
give You a break and some slack.

don't expect to love another
if Your own love isn't accepted
by Your own self.

it is not wrong of You to do so.

RED CARPET SKIN

best tailored suit,
ready to show off.

large hoodie and sweatpants,
ready to binge my show.

this is how my skin feels,
in anything at any time.

confident in me,
comfortable in me,
loving me.

RITUAL

sitting by fires,
warm and comforted.
you gave me this once.

but flames can burn
wounds that are slowest to heal.
you gave me this, too.

so i made my own and set myself ablaze,
to watch those lonely troubles
blow away with the cremated ashes
of my sad, former self.

i became one with the inferno,
my own warmth and comfort,
my own growing fire with dancing flames.

ABOUT THE AUTHOR

Hunter Summerall is a twenty-year-old artist and poet living in Los Angeles. Having deep roots in the entertainment industry, Hunter hopes to publish work that helps his readers feel less alone.

He can be found on Instagram and Twitter @huntersummerall.

It's a Lonely Love
copyright © 2018 by Hunter Summerall.
All rights reserved. Printed in the United States of America. No part
of this book may be used or reproduced in any manner whatsoever
without written permission except in the case of reprints in the
context of reviews.

Andrews McMeel Publishing
a division of Andrews McMeel Universal
1130 Walnut Street, Kansas City, Missouri 64106

www.andrewsmcmeel.com

18 19 20 21 22 BVG 10 9 8 7 6 5 4 3 2 1

ISBN: 978-1-4494-9588-6

Library of Congress Control Number: 2018946736

Editor: Katie Gould
Designer: Diane Marsh
Production Editor: Amy Strassner
Production Manager: Cliff Koehler

ATTENTION: SCHOOLS AND BUSINESSES
Andrews McMeel books are available at quantity discounts with
bulk purchase for educational, business, or sales promotional use. For
information, please e-mail the Andrews McMeel Publishing Special
Sales Department: specialsales@amuniversal.com.